God's ever-reaching guidance is calling from within us to bring us inner healing and peace...

Prologue

Our inner healing, inner guidance, and inner peace comes from God. It also comes from us because it is our birthright. We are created in the Image and Likeness of God, and that means that we have been built with everything we need to live healing, peace, and sound guidance.

We have just to remember who we are and to clear our space of the clutter that makes us forget.

This Journal is here as a resource and tool, so that you can remember who you are and in what Image you have been created.

We keep things in order for everyone. Our society, our bosses, our spouses, our children, our communities, our families, our neighbors, and our friends they all rely on us to keep it all together.

- What do we receive from keeping it all together for everyone else?
- What do we fear we will lose?
- What do we actually lose?
- What is the overall outcome of keeping things together for everyone else?

_____
_____
_____
_____
_____
_____
_____
_____
_____
_____

There are usually two responses when someone has a role placed on them, which they have not requested. One is to accept it without truly questioning it; another is to vehemently resist it.

- CAN YOU THINK OF WAYS AND TIMES WHERE YOU HAVE RESISTED WHAT IS NOT YOURS?
- CAN YOU THINK OF WHEN YOU HAVE ACCEPTED WHAT WAS THRUST UPON YOU?
- IS THERE A COMPASSIONATE WAY THAT YOU CAN LOVINGLY RELEASE WHAT YOU HAVE NOT REQUESTED?

When we allow our trauma to rename us, we live from that new name.

- Can you think of any trauma that you've lived through where you felt that who you were changed? An example of renaming might be: divorced, single-mom, college drop out or abandoned child.

If we identify ourselves as a victim, we take on the role and description of a victim.

- Can you describe how victims feel?
- Can you describe what victims do?
- Can you describe what other people think of victims?
- Does any part of you identify with being a victim?
- Does it make you feel empowered or exhausted?

_____
_____
_____
_____
_____
_____
_____
_____
_____
_____

Self-forgiveness and forgiveness of others frees us from the labels, identities, and the roles of a victim. It frees us from tying ourselves to the things that have been done to us.

- Take this time to cleanse out unforgiveness.
  - What happened? (Describe thoroughly what happened. Be open, honest, and raw in your description)
  - How did it make you feel? (Use the emotions chart found in Appendix 1. to help your describe your feelings)
  - What was your role/responsibility? [1]
  - What would you like to happen now? (Remember that you cannot change the past. It must be something attainable and achievable.)
  - Why you will forgive yourself?
  - Why you will forgive the other person?

_____
_____
_____
_____
_____
_____
_____
_____

---

[1] A note about knowing your role. We all play a role as though we are in a play. Sometimes it can be a very passive role, but it is important to know what your role was (is) in any situation. NOT to blame yourself, not always to take full responsibility, but just to understand and to describe where you stood (stand) in the "play" Also knowing your role does not mean that you must stop playing it, it is just important for you to know it. If you are to stop playing it, you will know after learning to be deeply in touch with your own voice.

Forgiveness frees us. It frees the next generation, too... Forgiveness is a gift to yourself.

- List some ways that you will feel more free if you can let go of something you do not want to forgive.
- What will your descendants gain if you let go of what you don't want to release.

_____
_____
_____
_____
_____
_____
_____
_____
_____
_____
_____

I grew up believing that following the Ten Commandments would lead me to heaven.

- List what you've heard about God, heaven, and sin.
- Explore whether the things you have been told seem achievable, freeing, and enjoyable.
- Do you feel restricted by what you have been told?

Jesus is giving us the key to life. He is commanding that we use our desire, our power, our thoughts, our words and our will for God.

- List ways that you use your desire, your power, your thoughts, your words, and your will for God.
- List ways that you use your power, your thoughts, your words, and your will for things not related to God.
- Can you think of creative and freeing ways to use more of you for God?

Before you can fulfill your purpose, you must discover it. Before discovering it, you must commit to the task of throwing off worldly instruction, labels, expectations, roles, and responsibilities.

- Can you think of any titles, labels, roles, expectations or responsibilities that you feel are keeping you from living out or finding your purpose?
- Are you willing to lovingly release anything that may be keeping you from finding and living your purpose?

...if the heart is filled with love, peace, joy, and happiness, it is filled with God.

- Is your heart filled with love, peace and joy?
- Name how the feelings of love, peace, and joy are connected to Godly thoughts and feelings.

Wherever you start in the process, either with searching yourself or searching God, you will arrive at loving yourself and loving God.

- What are ways that you have searched for God?
- Have they helped you learn more about you?
- What are ways that you have searched yourself?
- Have they helped you learn more about God?

When we refer to a heart being heavy, we are referring to the mind being overburdened and weighed down with worldly worries and concerns.

- IS YOUR HEART HEAVY OR OVERBURDENED RIGHT NOW?
- WRITE DOWN YOUR WORRIES AND CONCERNS.

The emotional trauma, in our DNA, needs to be released from our bodies through a heart connection.

- CAN YOU THINK OF WAYS THAT TRAUMA FROM YOUR ANCESTORS MAY BE SHOWING UP IN YOUR DNA?

_____
_____
_____
_____
_____
_____
_____
_____
_____
_____
_____
_____

She says having the disease forces women to halt. To connect. To have a Spiritual awakening in order to survive.[2]

- CAN YOU THINK OF ANYTHING IN YOUR LIFE, NOT NECESSARILY DISEASE, WHICH HAS FORCED YOU TO STOP, TO CONNECT, AND TO AWAKEN TO SPIRIT?
- AFTER THE CRISIS, DID YOU CONTINUE YOUR CONNECTION WITH GOD?
- HOW HAS IT CHANGED YOU GOING FORWARD?

---

2 (self-healing secrets.com)

Examining, cultivating, acknowledging, and changing what is loved, what is felt, and what is believed deep in your heart is the first step to loving God with "all your hearts."

- Have you acknowledged and examined what is in your heart today?
- What do you need to cultivate?
- What needs to be changed?

When we take the time to notice what is happening in our inner environment, we have the power to release what does not belong and to refuel with the Source of our being.

- What is your favorite way to take time to notice what is happening in your inner being?
- What is your favorite environment for getting still?
- When you check in and realize that you could release somethings, how do you do that?

Although we have heard the concept of God being Omnipresent (everywhere and in all things), we are constantly receiving images, messages, admonishments that God is away from us.

- When you think of God, where is he, she, it?
- Do you think that you are included in the "everywhere and in all things" when you think of where God is?

At this point deep inside, you bask in the love, peace, and creativity of God, and you can feel the truth in the scripture that says you are made in God's image.[3] *You can feel free, at peace, invincible, expansive, and completely open.*

- When you think of God, do you feel free, at peace, invincible, expansive, and open?
- If not, what is preventing you from feeling this way?
- Is there anything about what you have been taught about God keeping you from having an expansive and open relationship with she, he, or it?

_____
_____
_____
_____
_____
_____
_____
_____
_____
_____

[3] Genesis 1:27

The silence leads us to connection with the everlasting Source of God.

- How often do you allow silence in your life?
- When you take the time to become still what do you find?

He says being mindful of the breath is being mindful that God is in everything.[4]

- Do you believe that God is in everything?
- What does everything encompass?
- If you had to explain it, how would you say that the breath reminds you that God is omnipresent?

_____
_____
_____
_____
_____
_____
_____
_____
_____
_____
_____
_____

---
4 James Duncan

When we breathe, we are reminded of that place, that part of us where God resides.

- When you are silent, do you notice your breath?
- How deep are you breathing?
- How shallow?
- How fast is your breathing?
- How slow?
- Do you notice anything else when you notice your breathing?

_____
_____
_____
_____
_____
_____
_____
_____
_____
_____
_____
_____

Since God is in all of creation, and in everything, we should also acknowledge that God is in our bodies?

- Is God in your body?
- If so, how can you tell?
- If not, how do you know?

_____
_____
_____
_____
_____
_____
_____
_____
_____
_____

If God is in our bodies, then part of loving God with all our soul is to show love to and for our bodies.

- Are you showing your body love?
- Name ways that you could be more loving with your words toward your body.
- How can you be more loving with actions toward your body?
- How can you think more loving thoughts towards your body?

... the most damaging thoughts to health are those filled with criticism, anger, resentment, and guilt.

- ARE YOU EXPERIENCING ANY HEALTH PROBLEMS?
- ARE YOU ANGRY?
- ARE YOU RESENTFUL?
- DO YOU FEEL GUILTY?
- DO YOU FEEL CRITICIZED?
- ARE YOU CRITICAL OF YOURSELF?

_____
_____
_____
_____
_____
_____
_____
_____
_____
_____
_____

The body sends us signals and messages about our emotional state.

- IS YOUR BODY TELLING YOU ANYTHING ABOUT YOUR EMOTIONS?
- IS YOUR BODY ASKING YOU TO HEAL EMOTIONALLY?

Loving God using your might involves owning your God-given power.

- What does your God-given power look like?
- How do you wield your God-given power?
- How do you give your power away?

If one loses power by focusing on negative emotions, how does one gain power and might?

- WHAT IS YOUR PRACTICE FOR GAINING AND RECLAIMING YOUR POWER?

Mindfulness is taking responsibility, paying attention, self-monitoring, and showing yourself compassion.

- Do you have a mindfulness practice?
- If so, what does it look like?
- If not, do you need a mindfulness practice?

_____
_____
_____
_____
_____
_____
_____
_____
_____
_____
_____

In order for a woman to understand her might, and to use it for a greater purpose, she must understand her thoughts concerning God, herself, and her life.

- Is your understanding growing in the things of God?
- Is your understanding growing in the things of your inner self?
- Is your understanding growing in the things of your life and your path?

To understand your thoughts and beliefs, you have to pause. You have to set aside time and space to examine, breathe, and release.

- Have you set aside space to breathe?
- Are you examining your life? If so, how?
- Are you allowing yourself to lay down your burdens?
- How often?

_____
_____
_____
_____
_____
_____
_____
_____
_____
_____
_____

Your power lies in taking the time to hear God, and then to follow whatever path that leads you along. Only you and God know that path.

- Are you listening for God?
- Are you saying yes to what you hear?
- Are you obediently walking the path that you and God have created?

To love us and to understand our power, is to love God and to understand God-power. To love God and to partake of God-power is to love yourself and to empower yourself.

- Can you see that loving you is the path to God?
- Can you see that loving God is the path to you?
- Explore, explain, and expound on what you see?

Not having your thoughts in alignment with the truth of your God Imagery will lead you to a life where you feel you must measure up to the best worldly imagery.

- In what ways have you convinced yourself that you need to measure up?
- Do you need to measure up in your appearance?
- Do you need measure up in your intelligence?
- What about respect from the world?
- Achievements? Acknowledgements? Attachments?

You have to have faith to show up as love in a world which values unloving behavior.

- WHAT IS MOST FRIGHTENING ABOUT SHOWING UP IN THE WORLD AS LOVE?
- WHAT FEELS DISTRUSTFUL ABOUT BEING LOVING, LOVELY, LOVED, AND LOVABLE?
- WHAT DO YOU TRUST ABOUT BEING LOVING, LOVELY, LOVED, AND LOVABLE?

Draw your senses away from what you see in the world and go inside of yourself to find God's wisdom, love, acceptance, and peace.

- WHAT ARE YOU PRACTICING THAT FOCUSES YOU ON GOD'S WISDOM, LOVE, ACCEPTANCE AND PEACE?
- HOW OFTEN?

_____
_____
_____
_____
_____
_____
_____
_____
_____
_____
_____
_____
_____

Without taking care of ourselves first, we are unable to care for others in a healthy way. If we do not love ourselves, we are not giving true love to others.

- List the things you do for love.
- List the ways that you feel affection for others.
- Are the loving actions that you show linked to wanting to receive mutual feelings of affection?
- Are you loving others to receive love?
- Is there an alternative?

_____

_____

_____

_____

_____

_____

_____

_____

_____

_____

"*Jesus expected you to love yourself before loving others. Jesus suggested that loving yourself is the basis, the baseline from which you should give love to others.*" (LAMSA, Matthew 22:39)

- What did you learn about where you should place loving yourself as it relates to others?
- Does showing that you put others first make you feel like you are being Christ-like?
- Does God want you to put yourself last?

Showing ourselves love is the basis for making this world a loving place. We cannot love ourselves without knowing ourselves. We cannot know ourselves without exploring ourselves. Self-exploration is the foundation of self-love.

- WHAT IS YOUR PRACTICE FOR SELF-EXPLORATION?
- WHEN YOU EXPLORE YOU, ARE YOU EMBRACING WHAT YOU FIND?

The Bible states that we are made in the image and likeness of God. Male and Female, alike.[5] *Although, men may more closely align themselves with the image of God because they see pictures and movies of a male God, the Bible says that we are all created in God's image.*

- IF YOU WE ARE ALL CREATED IN THE IMAGE OF GOD, DESCRIBE HOW?
- IS PART OF GOD A WOMAN?
- IS GOD SPIRIT?
- IF I AM CREATED IN GOD'S IMAGE, DOES THAT MEAN THAT I HAVE GODLY DNA.

_____
_____
_____
_____
_____
_____
_____
_____
_____
_____
_____

---
5 Genesis 1:26, 27.

Many women have spent years not loving themselves. Sadly, religion has played a role in us not loving ourselves.

- DOES YOUR RELIGION CELEBRATE WOMEN?
- DOES YOUR RELIGION ENCOURAGE YOU TO COVER UP, DRESS UP, BE SILENT, BEHAVE, OR KNOW YOUR ROLE?
- IF YOU ARE ASKED TO HIDE YOURSELF, ALTER YOURSELF, OR SILENCE YOURSELF, CAN YOU LOVE YOURSELF TOO?

If you can believe that you are one with God when you go out into nature or a church, why can't you believe that you are one with God when you go into yourself?

- What in nature makes you feel God's presence and creativity?
- What about human cycles, expressions, and interactions are like nature?
- Can you see God in you, as in nature?

All we need is a daily remembrance that we are not separate from God. We are reflections of God. We already have God with us all the time.

- What reminds you that you are a part of God?
- What reminds you that God is a part of you?
- Are you separate from God?
- Does God ever need to be silenced, altered, or taught how to behave?

Would we treat people poorly if we recognized that they, like us, are all reflections of God. Would we love in a way that seeks to control others? Would we believe we own our mates, or our children, if we saw them as reflections of God?

Do we try to control God? Do we try to own God?

Do we treat God poorly?

... unity, connection, oneness.

- When you hear this what does it evoke?
- When you think about connection or oneness, with whom are you thinking of connecting?
- With whom would you achieve oneness?

Being able to recognize how we feel internally and externally leads us to our connection with God.

- How do you assess how you feel externally?
- How do you assess how you feel internally?
- How often do you take inventory of how you feel?

_____
_____
_____
_____
_____
_____
_____
_____
_____
_____
_____
_____

... a woman must be in touch with what arises from her soul by being familiar with herself.

- DO YOU KNOW YOURSELF WELL ENOUGH TO IDENTIFY WHEN YOU ARE BEING CALLED TO LIVE, LOVE, GIVE AND GROW?

We have needs that we suppress such as resting, mourning, laughing, reflecting, clarifying, and organizing. Being present helps us to address our needs.

- Have you been present for you inner self?
- What is your practice for being present?

My body is the pathway to self-evaluation. It is used to guide me, my emotions, my thoughts, and my purpose.

- How is your body a full participant in guiding emotions, thoughts, and purpose?
- How do you self-evaluate through the body?

_____
_____
_____
_____
_____
_____
_____
_____
_____
_____
_____

The body is our temple. A conduit for God's Spirit to move through us, speak through us, guide us, and to center us.

- Do you connect with the idea that the body is our temple?
- How do you treat your body like it is a place for God to use you?

Words matter. What a woman says and hears shapes her daily life and experience.

- Are you cultivating the environment that you see on a daily basis into what you want it to be in 5 years?
- Are you speaking words that create a beautiful life for yourself?

...lyrics and music can... make a woman feel supported and propelled to move forward.

- Do you have a playlist for your life?
- Is the music you listen to supporting you lyrically?

It is a means of processing emotions, raising the vibration, and finally moving into meditation in that elevated state.

- How do you process your emotions?
- How do you raise your vibration?
- How do you move into an elevated state of consciousness?

The foundation of compassion comes from growth and knowledge.

- WHAT QUESTIONS ARE YOU EXPLORING?
- WHAT KNOWLEDGE ARE YOU SEEKING?
- HOW OFTEN DO YOU SEEK AND QUESTION?
- DO YOU ALLOW WHAT YOU LEARN TO GROW YOU?

Sometimes, we think that we are being loving by being nice, and that is enough... Nice is not necessarily loving, honest, respectful, caring, or open. Nice is just about operating within a boundary that does not cause waves or that does not make problems.

- EXPLORE WAYS THAT YOU HAVE BEEN NICE, BUT NOT LOVING.
- EXPLORE WHY BEING NICE IS REQUIRED BY OTHERS?
- WHAT ARE THE CONSEQUENCES OF NOT BEING NICE?

Love comes from within. Being devoted to humanity and to love may require making the masses feel uncomfortable.

- Can you think of instances where love makes others feel uncomfortable?
- Why does love for humanity make people uncomfortable?
- Are you willing to reach for the love of humanity, even if you knew it would make your loved ones uncomfortable?

Practicing love and devotion is not necessarily a path lined with money and material possessions. We have been told that the acquisition of worldly things is synonymous with living a great life; with being successful.

- Is it possible to practice love and devotion for the world while acquiring worldly things?
- Is what we manifest an indication of the great life we have?
- If you died tomorrow would the way you loved be remembered?
- Would your possessions be talked about at your memorial?

The more we practice loving humanity and walking a path of devoted truth, the less we will rely on things associated with ego.

- What are the things associated with ego?
- If you thought of ego as "easing God out," how would you say that ego shows up in our lives in more way than just arrogance and pride?

Many of us know that the hungry need to be fed or that we should visit a sick person. We know that a poor person needs a hand and that an elderly person could use some help. But many people actually do nothing about it.

- Have you found a way to offer help, love, money, or time to those in need?
- How often do you involve yourself with assisting others?

Comparisons and judgements of one's self and of others begin to fall away when we can quiet the inner chatter in our minds.

- What is your practice for quieting your inner worry, fear, doubt, judgments, and resentment?
- How often do you practice?

The word silence or quiet is mentioned [in the Bible] often as a means for gaining strength, clarity, and purpose.

- Do you get still?
- What do you find when you quiet your mind?
- How do you hear God above the noise?

...afraid of different religions, different people, different ideas, and different philosophies.

- WHAT IS YOUR PRACTICE FOR DISPELLING FEAR RELATED TO DIFFERENCES?
- HOW DO YOU NOTICE WHEN YOU ARE AFRAID OF DIFFERENCES?
- WHY DO DIFFERENCES EXIST?

In the Bible, it says that God seeks to dwell in the person who is calm.[6]

- WHAT IS YOUR PRACTICE FOR CALM?
- WHAT IS YOUR PRACTICE FOR FEELING AT PEACE?
- DOES BEING CALM REMIND US THAT GOD DWELLS IN US OR DOES IT ATTRACT GOD TO US?

---

6 Isaiah 66:2

If it brings you discomfort, uneasiness, shame, or fear, do not practice it.

- DOES WHAT YOU PRACTICE ON A DAILY BASIS BRING YOU FEAR?
- DO YOU FEEL LIKE YOU NEED TO MEASURE UP?
- DO YOU FEEL SHAME OR GUILT AFTER YOU PRACTICE?

The breath has the power to cleanse stress, disease, tension, and emotional blockages.

- How often are you allowing yourself to breathe?
- What methods do you use to breathe away stress, tension, and blockages?
- Do you notice a difference in yourself after you take a breath?

Many times, we feel anxious about the future or regret over the past.

- Can you be fully present if you are concerned about the future and the past?
- What are you missing in the present when you are mentally experiencing the past and the future?

If a woman continuously practices devaluing the past, devaluing herself and others because of the past, eventually, her body will respond by supporting her feelings.

- WHAT WAYS DOES THE BODY PARTICIPATE WITH FEELINGS?
- WHAT WAYS DOES THE BODY RESPOND TO FEELINGS OF BEING DEVALUED?

_____
_____
_____
_____
_____
_____
_____
_____
_____
_____
_____
_____

Viewing things through a negative lens keeps you unhappy.

- What is the value in viewing anything that feels uncomfortable, unpleasant, and distressing through a negative lens?
- What is the value in believing that all experiences have positive impact?

Staying in the present and in full appreciation of it can immediately release happy hormones in the body.

- When you search this present moment, what do you find?
- Spend some time appreciating this moment. Search everything and anything in this moment to appreciate.

Fixating and fretting over things which have not occurred, keeps us from staying in the now.

- WHAT ARE YOUR CONCERNS FOR THE FUTURE?
- WHAT ABOUT THE PAST GIVES YOU ANXIETY ABOUT THE FUTURE?
- WHAT FIXATING THOUGHTS KEEP YOU FROM BEING HERE RIGHT NOW?

Understand that your feelings and bodily sensations are there to signal you. They are there to alert you about whether you are fully present or living in fear or regret.

- What do things like a headache, a backache, or tight shoulders tell you about yourself?
- What action do you take from what you are told?
- What do your feelings tell you about yourself?
- What actions do you take based on your feelings?

...to become familiar with God's voice. You must get quiet and listen for it. You must become familiar with it.

- Do you spend most of your conversation with God talking?
- Are you familiar with God's voice?
- Do you take the time to hear it?
- How often?

Notice what you are thinking. Notice what is running through your head. Notice it without judgement.

- Do you have a practice of noticing what is happening in your thoughts?
- Can you hear your thoughts with compassion?
- Can you be an observer of your own inner being?

The Mind, Body, and Spirit are connected metaphysically. Our bodies respond to what is happening in our Spirits and minds.

- Can you think of an illness that has happened to you after an emotional or mental incident?
- Are you speaking and believing life-affirming words to your body?

We are accustomed to caring for the emotions of others and taking on the burdens of others. When it comes time to really getting in touch with our emotions we do not know how to do it.

- Do you have a practice for taking care of your emotions?
- What happens to your burdens?
- When you feel overburdened, what do you do?

There are many practices to choose from...What is important, is that you choose one that speaks to your inner yearnings.

- Are you in communication with yourself?
- Can you articulate what you yearn for?
- What is it?
- Are you apart from it? Why?

_____
_____
_____
_____
_____
_____
_____
_____
_____
_____
_____

Whatever path you take, it is important to try many different modalities and to do something everyday.

- What is in your practicing toolbox to:
    - Stay present
    - Get in touch with God
    - Listen to your body
    - Quiet your mind
    - Live, Love, Give, & Grow

Bibliography

Duncan, James "'Pray Always': Breathing in God's Creative Energy." National Catholic Reporter. 48:4 (2011) 6a -7a. Print

Hopkins, Misa http://self-healingsecrets.com/1008/women's-rhythms-and-healing-autoimmune-diseases/ March 10, 2011.

1957, Bible English. Lamsa. Holy Bible from the Ancient Text: George M. Lamsa's Translation from the Aramaic of the Peshitta. San Francisco, CA: Harper & Row, 1968. Print.

Hay, Louise. Heal Your Body: The Mental Causes for Physical Illness and the Metaphysical Way to Overcome Them. March 7, 1995. Kindle Edition

About the Author

Rev. Dr. Brooke Brimm is a New Thought metaphysical women's practitioner.

She has devoted herself to ministering to the Mind, Body, & Spirit. Her advanced degree in Professional Counseling, certification in yoga, & a ministerial doctorate in Holistic Life Counseling/Metaphysics have given her the tools she uses to lead others to their inner healing, inner guidance, and inner peace. You can find her teaching at retreats, conferences, workshops, and weekly in classes which are on-line and in-person.

Brooke has authored two books: *Loves God Herself: Yoga and Mindfulness for Black Women Who Follow The Christ* & *Love's Gumbo: Ingredients for a Loving and Lasting Relationship*, both of which can be found on Amazon.

She has developed powerful spiritual programs which inspire women to explore and discover their authentic God-selves. They include her signature programs *Inner Beat Movement ™*, *Release the UnYou and Live as the Real You™*, and *Brooke Brimm Retreats™*. She is also the Founder of the non-profit organization 501(c3), **Brooke Brimm Ministries.**

BrookeBrimm.com

Made in the USA
Las Vegas, NV
26 December 2020